© 2019 by **Christie Black-Murrell**

Publishing Company
C. Black Expressions, INC

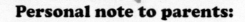

Personal note to parents:

As a counselor I have been witness to how powerful words of a parent can be on the life of a child. Their words can build a child up or tear a child down. Be careful how you use your words parents. It is essential to their design that you sow words of life into them. It will be those words that you speak that will give them the strength to stand up to bullies, believe in themselves, walk away from unhealthy friendships, and be the compassionate, smart, self-reliant children and young adults you want them to be.

You have a
Smart brain.

You will live
by faith.

You will move
mountains.

You are
So loved.

You were created for greatness!

You are
God's perfect
design.

Your smile is contagious.

Your future is bright.

You are
multi-gifted.

You have a
kind heart.

You are
independent.

You are
So brave.

Parents, now you have the chance to write personal positive affirmations for your child or children

1.

2.

3.

4.

5.

The praise of others is powerful, but the love of self builds strength...Write a few positive self-affirmations

1.

2.

3.

4.

5.

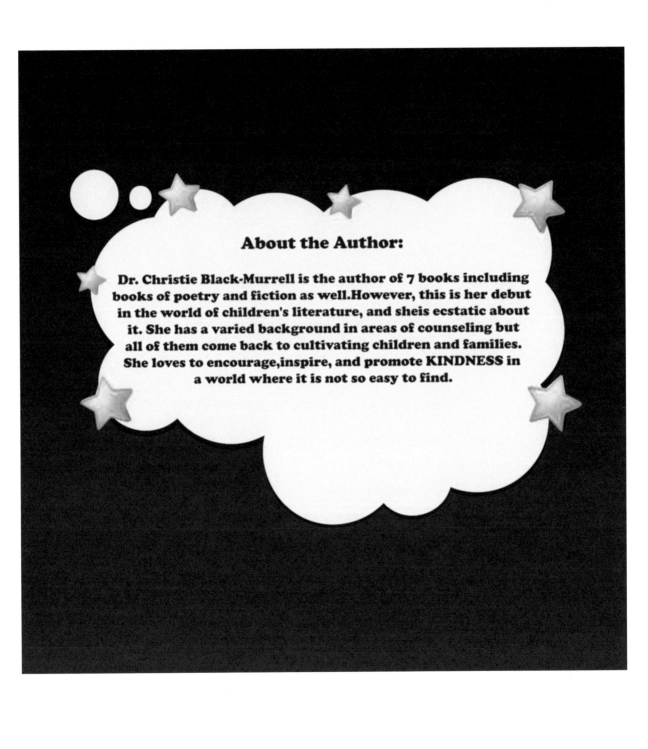

About the Author:

Dr. Christie Black-Murrell is the author of 7 books including books of poetry and fiction as well.However, this is her debut in the world of children's literature, and sheis ecstatic about it. She has a varied background in areas of counseling but all of them come back to cultivating children and families. She loves to encourage,inspire, and promote KINDNESS in a world where it is not so easy to find.

Made in the USA
Columbia, SC
17 November 2024